Spiritual

My Journey

Your Quest

Revd Christopher Morgan

Preface and Dedication

Someone recently asked me who this book is for. It talks a lot about me, and So it could fall into the genre of a true-life story, having said that it's not really exciting enough to be placed in the *true-life* category. There is quite a lot in this book about God, so it could appeal to those who are religious, but then again it challenges so many traditional religious views that it may annoy the religious reader. It is actually written for the vast majority of beautiful people in this world who want to think about God and Spirituality outside of formalised religion. Ordinary people who want to connect in a way that is meaningful, rather than sign up to something, which demands adherence to things they cannot fully accept. It is about freedom of mind, freedom of expression and non-conformity.

I have deliberately chosen to write in plain, every day English. I have made a conscious effort to avoid religious jargon and terminology. I have also deliberately avoided using "proof texts" to back up my arguments and observations. Some might suggest that this is because my approach is unorthodox, contradictory, and even heretical. They are entitled to their opinion. I will say that I am writing about spiritual and emotional connections, something which no science, whether secular or theological can offer evidence for except, perhaps in some small way within the realms of psychology.

I write for the ordinary person seeking a meaning to life.

When sitting down to write this book, I took the decision to name very few people who have shared my life's journey. There is good reason for this.

This book is not really about me, it's about helping others through sharing some aspects of my own journey to discover God for themselves and to break free from religious practices that constrict rather than give life. Coupled to this is the very fact that sometimes I have hurt others along the way, others have caused me pain and hurt too. It is not fair to identify and name those whose lives I am no longer a part of, neither is it fair on them to discuss what went wrong and why. Where an interaction or relationship is a necessary part of the story, it is mentioned in passing, but only in passing.

This book is dedicated to many people who have been a part of my journey,
I can't name them all, some have no name in my memory, they are just the result of passing conversations, or a one liner in a long forgotten book, some would not wish to be named. I have therefore chosen to dedicate this little book to significant contributors. It is dedicated in particular to the following who have played more than a meaningful role in my path this far.

To Jenny, who introduced me to God in the first place. Although our paths have been very different it was her influence that began it all.

To my dear, sorely missed Mum, who now knows what lies beyond, for giving me life.

To Father Nicholas, whose influence and deep spirituality continues to enrich my Ministry.

To my children who have helped me to learn what love is and who have
enabled me to understand that life is never black and white.

And finally to my soul mate, my dearest friend, the love of my life, Natasha who has taught me more than I can ever know, supported and guided me in so many ways. Most importantly she has taught me that religious dogmas and platitudes are never an answer to life's deepest questions.

About the Author

Christopher is a Community Chaplain ministering across faiths and denominations throughout the East of England.

Married to Natasha, they have seven children between them. Natasha is a Priest in the Church and works to bridge the gap between traditional Christianity and Spiritualism, combining both approaches in her own journey.

Christopher is General Secretary of the Society for Peace and Prior of the Grove of Solitary Christian Druids. He also works a Funeral Director and bereavement supporter.

Between them, Christopher and Natasha offer spiritual guidance and support to any that seek it.

This is my simple religion. There is no need for temples; no need for complicated philosophy. Our own brain, our own heart is our temple; the philosophy is kindness.

Dalai Lama

Beginnings

I don't think that I have ever been conventional. My earliest memories are of
being somehow different to the other children. I never felt comfortable following the crowd or conforming to convention.

The "why" debate sticks in my mind. I must have been 7 or 8, and on a rare family occasion was out shopping with Mum and Dad somewhere in London. Chatting away as I always did, I can't recall what the conversation was about, I asked my father "why", no doubt in the profound way that a 7 or 8 year old asks such questions. Dad, presumably must have answered with something, as I recall that I continued to challenge every answer with "why" until we reached a point when I was advised firmly that the conversation had come to an end. Now, as a parent and grandparent myself, I have experienced that moment when a somewhat annoying child realises that they can continue to ask, "why", if anything just to get the upper hand and annoy Dad! Knowing me, there was no doubt an element of that innocent wickedness involved, but also I suspect there was a real and genuine thirst for a credible answer, something which I recall I wasn't' given.

My childhood was a fairly nomadic existence, due to my father's work. Although much of it was spent what would now be just inside the M25 motorway. Mum was a lapsed Irish Catholic, actually lapsed is too soft a word, she had embraced atheism as I suspect a reaction to pre Vatican II Romanism, and the blind and prevalent hypocrisy that she had experienced.

A women of no describable faith but one whom to her dying day had a clear understating of right and wrong, of morality and of the commandment to "love your neighbour". To use the old cliché, she would do anything for anyone, and despite her and I having an occasionally tempestuous relationship in my late teens and early 20's, I remember her as a good and deeply caring woman who would live out what might be described a Christian life, only without the God bit! Dad was and is, like so many nominally Church of England. Dad too has no time for hypocrisy, but does have a deep seated but quiet faith.

It was into this warm, loving, if disjointed family due to dad's work that I entered the world in the January of 1966. I was the eldest child (I had to wait for 9 years for my sister to arrive) and so I craved all the attention, was given all the attention and I LOVED it. By all accounts I was not an easy child – a bit of a live wire and behaved beyond the reassuring parameters of the textbook "stages" that we all go through. I remember from my earliest days being outside, leaping over the garden fence and disappearing into the woods, playing by the canal, and even IN the canal on occasion. One story that illustrates my desire to be outside is that one morning Mum and Dad were awoken to a knock on the door at 5 am. I had been found out playing in my pyjamas and wellies, I was only around 4 years old at the time – I had

somehow escaped, unlocking the front door whilst my parents slept. Another time I had convinced myself that holding a
feather in each hand would be sufficient for me to fly, and so prised open my bedroom window to give it a go and soar with the birds. My father came in to my room and put a stop to my scheme just in the nick of time – I might not be writing this now if he hadn't. I was constantly wanting to be outside,
exploring, imagining, and importantly problem solving. Problem solving, however was not just an outdoor pursuit. Many a time I awoke fancying a midnight snack, and my parents, finding that a kitchen raids were taking place, took ever-increasing measures to thwart the nocturnal burglar (me). A family story tells of how Mum and Dad locked the hatch from the dining room to the kitchen from the inside (my favourite point of entry, I am told) and then for good measure sprinkled flour on the floor in order to catch me, if not in the act, but to give enough evidence to show that it was me. Even I don't know how I did it, but I still managed to find a way in, avoid the flour and have my feast....I think they gave up after that.

This ability to "find a way around a problem", has been both advantageous and of course a cause of getting my fingers burned as life has gone on and I still, to this day often proclaim that there is no such thing as a problem, every mountain, no matter how high can be overcome, somehow. There is, however another area of my own approach to life that mirrors this problem solving philosophy, alongside the great "why" conversation. It's the "R" word – religion. Religion and Spiritual paths present to the small child in me a never-ending supply of "whys" and hatches locked from the inside.

God, Religion and Jedi's

God didn't feature in my earliest days, I was too busy exploring the world around me and displaying the type of hyperactivity that exhausted my parents on a daily basis. I knew something about a little boy who was born on Christmas day, but his story was very much secondary to the fact that I was showered with presents which brought so much excitement that one year I sneaked downstairs, opened everyone else's, wrapped them up again and to my delight announced to each person what they were unwrapping – I thought it was great fun. There was the other bloke who died one Friday, and because of that I was given access to a day gorging on chocolate a couple of days later. Why I couldn't have the chocolate on the day he died, I never worked that out, but there we are I munched through my eggs anyway. Its important at this juncture to point out that my parents were neither undisciplined nor did they approve of my gay abandon approach to these two significant days. I think they simply gave up trying to calm me into some sort of structure and decorum!

The first time this God person became a feature for me was when a new family moved in next door. David, Joyce and Jenny have remained lifelong friends, despite the fact that our paths have taken very different directions.

They had this God bloke living in their house! They spoke to him, thanked him for their meals and talked about him all the time. Mum and Dad, David and Joyce all became great friends and Jenny became a daily playmate. My recollection is that we had at that time similar temperaments, although of course she was far better behaved than me (despite ensuring that the end of my little finger was chopped off by the lid of a piano!). I have fond memories of playing together, getting into scrapes and carefree days. I have fond memories too of Jenny introducing me to this God person. Apparently he was very nice, he loved me no matter what I did. This was great news for a wild 5 year old...I could do anything and he would just forgive me! Jenny confirmed that this was indeed the case. He also made me, even though I protested that I had somehow appeared from Mummy's tummy, and I when I die I won't die because I will live forever in heaven. Oh how I wish sometimes that a time machine was in existence, just to go back and witness this beautiful, innocent conversation between two children. Jenny, the evangelist and little Christopher the live wire. I have so much to thank Jenny for, she started the ball rolling. I was her first "conversion" and although she has stayed true to her path ever since, and I have journeyed in a different direction, I doubt whether I would have even stepped foot on the path at all if it wasn't for her.

So, at 5 or 6 I had the God bug. Not that it made any real difference, my behaviour was still challenging, I still drove my mother around the bend, being all sweetness

and light to my father and other relatives. Although this God thing had caught me, there was a problem. Even at 5 it meant conforming to something. For Mum and Dad it meant a potential oasis in addition to school. They could get rid of me on a Sunday morning – they could send me to Sunday School! So I went, I injected my usual sense of fun into the proceedings and on one occasion was threatened for doing so with
expulsion. It kept me off the streets I suspect and out of Mum's hair.

Little changed between the ages of 5 and 11. I grew a bit older, I quietened down a little, and we moved around, I even experienced a few months living in Berlin. This move had its moments too. I developed a fear of Alsatian dogs (still with me today) on account of having been forced to watch a film about the dangers of rabies starring Mutley the mouth foaming Alsatian. My first exploration of my new surroundings in Berlin involved being chased by an Alsatian, which resulted in my expressing my anger to its owner by presenting him with a "Heil Hitler" salute and goose stepping away, only for him to let go of the dog's collar whilst uttering something incomprehensible in German, my final words as I scaled a fence and got the better of the raging dog was, "we won the war you know"! I don't know whether our time in Berlin was cut short (we were only there for 3 months) due to the official reason of a promotion for Dad or whether it was felt that getting this child back to England where he could at least not make offensive

remarks to the natives might not be a bad thing! I have been assured it was
Dad's promotion.

Perhaps the most significant event was the birth on my sister in 1975. I'd always wanted a sister, and loved babies. She was beautiful, I absolutely adored her and she changed my world. She probably had a bit of a calming influence on me. She was more of a conformist; she was lively, funny, always smiling and so beautiful, but far less of a live wire than her big brother. I suspect that inside my head, I now had a responsibility, I was the big brother, I was there in the park to shout "Oi" at other little children who tried to take her dolly away, I was a hero, and I liked that.

On the God front, I am not sure whether anything particularly grew. I discovered that the baby at Christmas and the bloke at Easter were one in the same, although it didn't dampen my approach to either festivity. I learned a few hymns, how to say the Lord's Prayer, and had discovered too that there was another option after death, the place where naughty people go. In my mind this was confusing. If God loved me unconditionally, then surely he loved everyone the same, so why was there a naughty pit called hell. I suspected that this was for the ultra bad people.

One Easter holiday, in an attempt to be rid of me for an entire week, Mum and Dad sent me to "Bible Class", I was 7. Everything was explained to me, in particular

what it is to "know" Jesus. All of us said that we knew him, but we were advised that we knew "of" him, to know him we had to enter into a personal relationship, give our lives to him, forever, and then we would be guaranteed a place in heaven. Refusal to do so meant eternal damnation. So, there was no real debate in my mind and when we are asked who wanted to give their lives to Jesus on the last day of the holiday club, after checking
that I was not alone, my hand shot up (mainly because everyone else had and I didn't want to look silly, plus they all got free Bibles and sweets for doing so – a further incentive). I was now a Christian and going to heaven!

Looking back my spiritual experiences were incredibly limited. A religious building was called a church, and it was generally old and musty. It was looked after by a vicar, who again was generally white, middle class, old and always a man. The vicar had services one day each week, hymns were sung and prayers were said. The rest of the week was nothing to do with the church type God.

So I developed my own weekday God. I met Him, always him, and spoke to him when I was out in the woods, playing by the canal, running through fields. I used to talk to that God quite a lot because he was real and tangible.

He wasn't old, didn't smell musty and I could talk to him in my own way without the thee's and thou's. I didn't have to sing to him or kneel down when I spoke to him. I didn't realise at the time but what I had learned was to see God in things other than manmade religion and its trappings. For me God wasn't omnipresent, how could he be? You can't be in two places at once!

God instead popped up, quite a bit in my case, rarely in church, but often when I was out and close to nature. He did, however become very present and real in one particular church, Canterbury Cathedral, which became an important spiritual place for me as the years went by, but it was only at Canterbury Cathedral, amongst all churches, that I found him. Within those ancient walls he was quite different, a more formal God who expected hymns and kneeling and long services. Despite my natural antagonism to such things, he was strangely close. I spent many hours exploring, imagining, praying, and connecting in that great cathedral which even to this day remains a place of deep significance. Looking back I suspect that what I had created was three Gods, not even three facets of God, as each had a distinct
role. There was the god of the trees, the forests, the mountains, the seas – he was my best friend, the best friend I ever had. He allowed me to be me, wanted me to be me and expected nothing in return. Then there was the God of Sunday School and church, he was the "parent God", the one who told me off, kept me on the straight and narrow and beckoned me to conform.

Finally there was the gentle "Grandfather God" who resided in Canterbury Cathedral, he would show me things, connect me to the past, he was old and wise, demanded respect, but not in the disciplinarian way that the "parent God" did.

From the age of 11 things changed significantly. My Religious and Spiritual journey became more streamlined, my relationship with nature less so, with the exception of the sea which became significant. From this age onwards my natural personality, being an individual, not conforming was under sustained attack. These were dark days, but with tangible rays of light.

In the September of 1977 my childhood ended. I was only 11, and so still had some childhood in me, but the life I had known to this point disappeared the moment my parents drove me through the gates of the boarding school which was to be my home, with the exception of holidays for the next five hellish years.

The school was, and still is, nestled 2 miles or so from Dover Castle, overlooking the English Channel in the distance and further afield, on a good day, the coast of France. I had prepared myself for this move by reading the schoolboy tales of "Jennings", set in a 1950's prep school. It all sounded good fun. It wasn't. For the first time in my life I had to share a room with 12 other people, I had always had my own room before, and this was quite a difficult concept. At 8pm, dressed in pyjamas, we knelt beside our beds whilst a fearsome housemaster said prayers, and at 8:30 it was lights out, and complete silence. Not a word could be uttered, even

the whimpers of home sick boys were not allowed. The penalty for breaking silence was the slipper. My parents had always been clear on discipline, they had to be with me, but I can count on the fingers of one hand the times when the ultimate punishment, a smack, was given. They disproved of slippers, canes and belts, but this new institution did not and corporal punishment was handed out liberally, and publicly. As I became more homesick, I found that I had other boys teasing me, this made me more tearful. I wasn't used to this
combination of deep emotion, and the more I cried, the more I was bullied.

Very quickly this noisy, talkative, headstrong live wire was reduced to a deeply shy, insecure and tearful shadow of his former self as a combination of bullying and unwarranted corporal punishment took its toll. Physical and mental abuse, as we would now describe it was rife, and a number of us were victims of other forms of abuse, myself included, although thankfully on only one occasion.

If there is a hell, then I was experiencing it. At night I would lie awake and think about how I might get home, of course the penalty for doing so was to be brought back, given six strokes of the cane, and then expelled. Mum wouldn't bring me back, would she? I asked to go home, I cried down the 'phone and wrote passionate letters saying how unhappy I was, but they all fell on deaf ears, or so I thought. I found in later years that my parents were very sympathetic to my plight, and very concerned about my welfare, but it was deemed a good school and the hope was that I would eventually settle in. I did eventually, and now after the passage of time have some fond memories, but these are few and far between. I couldn't wait for the day when I could finally walk out of the place.

I have always enjoyed reading other people's stories. It doesn't matter whether they are famous or not. The one thing that has always interested me is how in the face of adversity human beings have a way of finding that chink of light to latch onto, that momentary glimmer of hope, a way of getting through adversity.

The private school system of the late 20th century was a bastion of cruelty and depravity. Devoid of love, boys and girls either adapted and made the best of things, or they lived a miserable existence in constant fear of bullying and abuse from teachers and other children. I fell into the latter category. Because my self-esteem had been damaged and I had become quiet and insecure, I found it even harder to make friends, I had fallen into the worst trap in this system, I showed weakness, and thus was bullied all the more.

I could write a book describing the way in which so called caring adults structured and ran such institutions. Those of us who went through it know, and some of the worst excesses are only now being brought to light and taken seriously as society faces up to its apathy of 30 plus years ago. My heart sinks to a point of tears when I see a parent publicly chastise a child, whether the child deserves to be told off or not. I have seen boys being beaten with sticks, being hit so hard with cricket bats that there is a cracking sound as the bat meets with their body. I have seen the deep black bruises on the buttocks of boys who have been thrashed with the sole of a gym shoe, and the cuts on the outer thigh from the whip lash of a cane, and it will never leave me. I have seen much, much worse given out by those caring for other people's children. I could go on, but instead I want to try to focus on the positives. In a strange way, experiencing what I experienced has made me who I am today. Being deprived of love has enabled me to learn what love is. Witnessing and being on the receiving ends of all sorts of abuse at the hands of adults and other children has made me understand that there is a better way of living, that violence and abuse, however subtle has no place in a society or world where love is spoken of, and most importantly that fear and misery is never the way to keep others in line.

I had to find my chinks of light, and realised that there were three things I enjoyed, which I could readily access and which would ultimately get me through. Two of these would inevitably lead to more ostracisation and bullying by the majority, but the trade off was worth it, the other, no one ever needed to know about.

The first of these three was the sea (and the one that only I knew about). Only a 45-minute walk away from the school gates was the vast expanse of the English

Channel. The ebb and flow of the sea, the gentleness contrasted by its destructive force fascinated me. It mirrored human nature, exceeded human nature; it enveloped, washed, sustained and destroyed life. I could sit on the beach for hours just watching and being at one with the waves, a deeply spiritual experience even at the age of 11, and it connected me with God. The problem for me was twofold. Firstly in the junior part of the school where I spent the first couple of years two years, we were only allowed out on a Saturday and Sunday afternoon, and only in two or more. Secondly, We had to wear our best uniform, which would make us conspicuous to others. Even on those occasions when we were allowed to wear something different, i.e. a school tracksuit for trips out in the countryside it was a still school tracksuit and so we stuck out like sore thumbs! I wanted anonymity, I craved solitude in a system where I couldn't even shower behind a screen, I wanted to be with God as I met him in the sea, alone, he was my God, and I needed to find a way to get to the coast on my own, and wearing something that was not going to make me conspicuous.

Bribery was rife in my school, passing on a few pennies to someone to keep them quiet generally worked on the basis that there was mutual benefit and that we both had something tangible on each other if either party was tempted to squeal. One of my dormitory peers, a 13 year old had found himself a girl friend and on a couple of occasions had asked me to "sign out and in" with him, looking as if we were off to Dover together. Generally speaking I was then left for a few hours whilst he went off with his girl friend, not the best of plans, an 11 year old sitting alone in the local museum waiting for someone to return from their romantic escapade. I was questioned a couple of times (we were supposed to be in twos at all times) and the excuses, which generally were, "he's gone to the toilet, a bit constipated, so has been some time" started to wear thin. When I told him that I could no longer cover for him in this way I was advised in very strong terms that if I didn't I would pay the price, a beating for being disloyal. And so, a bit of the old me emerged from the shadows, I wanted so much to be alone with my God, the sea, he wanted to be with his girl friend, and so I made him an offer that he couldn't refuse. I would hand over my entire 25 pence pocket money and in return I would sign out with him and then, once out of sight go off and do my own thing, meeting later at the prescribed time to sign back in together. He agreed, and following the first half term break, armed with the other part of my plan our once a week scheme fell seamlessly into place.

Once out of the main school gates it was a right turn to town or a left turn towards the sea. There was very quickly a bend in the road, which obscured us from the watchful eyes of the gatekeeper and was fortunately next to a small wood with a track out towards the cliffs and of course the sea. Once in the woods, I would remove my uniform to expose my "civilian" clothing and conceal my school uniform in a tree hollow. By this time,

my partner in this plan was already a long way down the road and I could then head for
the cliffs, and eventually down to the sea at St. Margaret's Bay for my weekly fix. How this scheme was never foiled I will never know, perhaps God was somehow assuring that all went well. On a couple of occasions we were "gated", the term meaning that we were not allowed out, I still found a way out, through a hole in the fence, a bit of bribery again and I was with God lapping against the seashore.

I had always enjoyed singing. The school had a well-established choir and after the first half term we were invited to apply to join. The choir master, a cathedral standard Organist, with a balding head, black national health glasses and trousers with the waistline just under his breasts was one of the very few teachers who showed any form of kindness. Coupled to which the former rather austere school chaplain had retired and his successor was
keen to offer boys in the choir tea and biscuits at his home on a Sunday evening, an oasis in what I was begin to feel was nothing more than a concentration camp for boys.

So I joined up, and this was to be the highlight of my school career, the choir, the weekly prayer meetings at the chaplain's house, alongside of course my weekly visits to my own holy place, the sea, were what got me through. Indeed, the positivity of these three things combined was such that on one of the darkest occasions ever, which I have never spoken of before, standing at 2 am in the shower block with my dressing gown chord around my neck, momentarily about to jump from a pile of books and end it all, a small but tangible voice in my head said "no" and I felt a sense of warmth and love as I heard choral singing, with the sound of waves lashing against the background of my mind. I untied the chord, replaced the books and crept back to bed.

Mum and Dad had chosen not to have me baptised as an infant, they felt I should be able to make up my own mind. Of course singing in the choir left me exposed to a considerable amount of Christian material and I felt, rightly or wrongly that I really should get myself dunked if I was to be a full choir member. The Baptism took place in the school chapel, to my delight the choir master, affectionately known to us as Reggie came along with a small number of my family, and I was allowed back to my Grandmother's house in Canterbury for an extended afternoon to celebrate with my family.

The following year, confirmation was offered and I signed up.

An important part of the process was the Confirmation classes. This took us away from the grind of boarding house life once a week, and added further ridicule to the fact that I was "wet", a "poof" etc. etc for being in the choir. Even worse – I was now a "Christian"! I didn't really care, I had by now grown an exterior shell, inside I was soft, hurting, shy, and desperate to reach 16, but they couldn't hurt the outside any more. One Sunday evening, our Chaplain took all the candidates out to the cinema.

The film? Star Wars.
I remember at the time thinking how cool the Chaplain was taking us to see such a film! There was method in his treating us, if formed the basis for a discussion about the Holy Spirit, or its Parallel in Star Wars, "The Force". I have to say that I have used this very film in the past myself when preparing candidates for confirmation during my time as an Anglican. You tube very nicely has the snippet where Luke Skywalker is told by OB1 to "use the Force" as he prepares to destroy the death star. It's a good talking point. For me though, at the time, the overriding thought process was not distinctly Christian but rather the eternal battle between good and evil, what is good, what is evil, and does any religion have the answers or monopoly on these things? Fairly deep thoughts of a boy of 13, but I didn't express them as I was too terrified of being ridiculed. I chatted to God about them when I visited him on the following Saturday, sitting cross-legged under a cliff isolated from any onlookers. He answered in his usual way through the ebb and flow of the water gently lapping upon the shore.

My confirmation was actually quite memorable; the Bishop was a ferocious and quite unsavoury character. He told us that we were all frauds and that almost none of us would keep our confirmation vows. After roaring "let us pray" and hearing the shuffling of 450 boys trying to settle down on their knees he screamed "STAND UP" and promptly told us that when we get down to pray we do so in silence...you could have heard a pin drop.

A few years later, still in the choir, still subject to constant ridicule and bullying, still living beneath that hard shell that had taught me that sometimes it is advisable to conform, if only for self preservation, I walked out of those gates for the last time. I remember crying, much to the annoyance of my mother who told me to stop blubbing, "You hated the place, what are you blubbing for". I was blubbing tears of joy, tinged with some sadness, sadness that I was leaving my beloved sea and my choir to enter the big wide world.

Guns, wanderings and conformity.

Looking back, I had absolutely no real idea what I wanted to do when I left school. At an early age I wanted to be one of Father Christmas's elves, a doctor, an airline pilot, a merchant seaman and even an undertaker. So, having spent the last five years of my life in a regime of terror, where freedom was non-existent and where the harsh discipline meant living in a constant atmosphere of fear I decided to join the Army! At the tender age of 16 I stepped off the bus at the Infantry Junior Leaders Battalion just outside Folkestone, in many ways to "do it all over again". Once again, I found solace in the sea, once again I found church and groups organised by the chaplain one of the few joys, and once again I found ways around the system. The only problem this time is that the British Army are rather better than crusty old school masters at finding out what errant soldiers are up to and so my charge sheet grew rather long during my time there. My list of "crimes" showed nothing serious, failing to clean my weapon, leaving camp when confined to barracks, that sort of thing. The worst was when I was given three days restrictions of privileges (a sort of military community sentence) which meant performing some menial task each day and turning up at the guardroom at 10pm to be inspected in best uniform. I had realised that the staff in the guardroom often didn't have a clue who was supposed to be there, so I just didn't bother. What I didn't know was that on day three my Corporal was on duty and he of course knew that I was supposed to be there. A "fair cop" as they say, and I experienced two days in a cell for my "crime", the only advantage of which was being fast tracked through the cook house queue at meal times! Not wanting to repeat the experience I behaved myself thereafter.

When the army and I eventually parted company I was discharged in a very unusual way. There are various categories relating to why a soldier is discharged. One of these is "services no longer required". This is normally reserved for someone who hasn't met the grade, or whose conduct hasn't been bad enough to warrant a dishonourable discharge but nevertheless in non army terms has been subject to some sort of disciplinary proceedings. Despite my rather lengthy charge sheet (most of which contained the same persistent offence – going absent on a Saturday afternoon without permission) I was marked with exemplary conduct. The Discharge papers read, "Morgan is an intelligent young man and in the right situation will be a huge asset. I am sure he will build a successful career at a senior level. However, he is a loner, who prefers the company of himself rather than being part of a team and thus unsuited to army life".

I look back at this time, actually with great fondness and some sense of pride. OK, I didn't do the two years that national servicemen endured up until the 1950's, but all in all I wasn't that far off and I left a fully trained soldier.

I also left as a pacifist, something the army and I failed to have a
conversation about, for obvious reasons! This was nothing to do with fear on my part but rather one of those defining moments, holding a loaded 7.62 SLR (Self loading Rifle) against my shoulder picking off the "enemy" with blank rounds whilst on exercise suddenly realising that this was not the way. Not the way to solve the world's problems, not the way to protect others, not the way to live the way of love. I realised that having a deterrent meant that everyone else needed a deterrent of equal or greater might, and that the never ending cycle of domination, control, suffering and death would continue.

I also had more pressing thoughts, I had a girlfriend.

My girlfriend was a Roman Catholic. I knew nothing about Catholicism except in terms of the negativity that existed as a hangover from the Reformation and still does to this very day. We spent many long hours talking about her faith and beliefs, I accompanied her to Mass, bought a Rosary and peered quizzically into the eyes of the statue of the Virgin in her church. The Priest was my sort of chap too. A chain-smoking whiskey drinking Irishman, we got on well, despite my not being one of "his". What hit me and appealed greatly was the ritual of it all, the deep symbolism, the bells, the smells and the fine vestments, it was awesome. I remember at the age of 18 telling my father that I was going to convert, I won't record his response, but I resigned myself to the fact that it was never going to be an option.

After leaving the army I returned home, my mother frog marched me from the train to the job centre (suitcase still in hand) and within 24 hours I had a job. I joined the village Church choir and settled, uncomfortably at first, into the freedom of non-institutionalised life for the first time in almost 7 years. I discovered beer, night clubs, cigarettes and the odd girl or two, and spent my days off lazing in the caravan my parents had borrowed to accommodate me, having reclaimed my bedroom when I joined the army and no longer having any room for me.

I got on well with our local vicar, a tall Yorkshire man who had been seized by the liberal movement at its height in the 1960's. A staunch supporter of the then Bishop of Durham whose academically literate truths were tabloid headlines, I learned much from him. I trundled along, doing all the things an 18/19 year old does, and more whilst singing in the church choir and attending the sorts of groups that kept me going at school and in the Army. I went to study groups, faith rallies, healing services etc., I also attended Mass regularly at the Cathedral Church in Northampton and befriended one of the elderly Priests who would privately teach me about "the faith" in his room after Mass with a strong coffee laced with not a small amount of Jamieson's.

I remember writing in my diary at the time that I was living a Jekyll and Hyde existence, I was enjoying being the real me, but the messages I was getting from Church circles were contradictory – I shouldn't be drinking, I shouldn't be smoking, I shouldn't swear, I certainly shouldn't be going too far with girls or allowing my late teenage urges to get the better of me.

Church and religion though felt comfortable and safe, I had a relationship with and an acute awareness of God, but all I knew was the circles I moved in. I remember one night asking for prayer after a bible study group to help me in an attempt to give up the fags. I hadn't smoked since the evening before and was having withdrawal symptoms. Within seconds I was having the demon of nicotine cast out of me, hands were laid upon me, there was shouting, wailing and praying in tongues, Jesus was constantly invoked and an hour later it was announced that the devil had left me. I was in a daze, something had happened. I left the chapel floating on air and promptly went to the pub to buy a pint of lager and 20 cigarettes. Jekyll and Hyde!
It's easier to be an individual in the real world, the world away from institutions, it's easier to be someone who doesn't conform and to hold your own views and as the days of my schooling and short army career became further behind me in my journey I also began to become very slowly more confident in being myself.

I was now married, a father with responsibilities, some of which I took seriously and others I failed miserably at.

To a certain degree I was able to be myself. Church was important to me, still, and although fatherhood had settled me down at least a little I still felt that my views and some aspects of my life were incompatible with the messages I was receiving about what being a Christian was all about. Having said that, I seemed to manage to pull it off, perhaps my early experiences of gaining access to the kitchen had taught me to work around a problem in ways that meant I could live what I believed to be a double life. It was either that this was the case and I needed to work harder at it or simply just be myself. Whatever the key to my success it, pulling off the public persona was all the more important, I had just reached the final interview stages to train as a Lay Reader (Preacher). I cycled the 7 miles to my interview clad in my tweed jacket, making sure I packed in as many cigarettes as possible before consuming three packets of extra strong mints and drenching myself with Old Spice aftershave – couldn't let the interviewers know I indulged in such a filthy habit, it wasn't something Preachers do of course!

I arrived in time for morning coffee, all part of the interview process, where we were observed interacting with each others. I was a fish out of water! I was in my early 20's, they were all 40 plus. They all spoke with eloquent "middle class" English, I was somewhere between ex-private schoolboy and cockney. They had been Christians forever, I hadn't a clue. They all had degrees, I could easily have had one, but just couldn't be bothered, and so stopped my education with "O" levels of which I had just four. They all talked about churchy things, I wanted to talk about my children.

It was a non starter, the interview was awful, my shyness got the better of me and a speech impediment that occasionally lays me low in times of extreme stress decided to return just as the interview started. Needless to say I was "not recommended for training". I was devastated, something inside told me that this was my path in life, but I hadn't met the academic grade, or any other of the criteria for that matter. I wasn't Christian enough, wasn't middle class enough, lived in a Council house was a civil servant of the lowest grade and was too shy to stand up in front of a group of people. I arrived on my vicar's doorstep in tears, "Jesus didn't ask his disciples to have degrees, a snooty accent and know all about the Bible," I said through the tears, " He just said, "Follow me"". " They are a bunch of stuck up bastards!" My vicar smiled, and said, "leave it with me". Two weeks later I was reading the lesson in church each Sunday, leading the prayers, I was being tutored by a retired priest in the rudimentary elements of Christianity, and a year later was leading Sunday School and family services when the vicar was on holiday. In the back ground, despite the fact that no one had advised me to do so, I packed up the fags, stopped swearing (well almost), managed to obtain a promotion at work and two years to the day of my rejection attended another selection conference, this time on my moped (I had gone up in the world). I returned home and waited...the news came through, I had been accepted!

The new, confident, non rebellious, conforming me had done it!

I embarked on my training with great gusto and in 1992 was admitted and licensed as a Reader in the Church of England, the youngest Reader by years in my own diocese, possibly one of the youngest in the Church of England. I had done it, I had answered the call, but at what cost. I now accepted and believed what I was taught to believe, and expounded it with great gusto from the pulpit. What was described as a more down to earth attitude and a bit of a twinkle in my eye seemed to warm my approach to many congregations – I was liked as well, for the first time in my life, not by one or two but by lots of people. I had matured, grown up, and finally accepted what my own religion was all about. I was far from liberal in my views, the Bible informed my beliefs. The sea still lapped against the shore many miles away but had little to do with me now, I had found God, or perhaps more truthfully I had, for whatever reason accepted a set of dogmas, many of which made no sense at all, rationally anyway, but I had learned the arguments!

As time went on more and more people talked about going forward for Ordained Ministry, the old fears arose, I'm not vicar material...but as more and more people suggested that I ought to explore that route, I realised that the only thing to do was to put myself forward and see what happened. It was a long process and in the background many life changes took place. By the time I reached the doors of my college in the University of Oxford to begin my pre Ordination training in 2002 I had even fulfilled my childhood ambition to become an Undertaker, a job that I continued alongside my studies until in July 2004.

In the same cathedral I was made a Reader 12 years before I arose from my knees as a Deacon. You may ask what went through my head on such a spiritual occasion, well; nothing very spiritual I'm afraid. As the Bishop removed his Ordaining hands from my head and motioned me to arise the character of Dell Boy from "Only Fools and Horses" rang out clearly in my head, "you've only gone and bloody done it!"

The Church of England is a funny institution. It claims to be both Catholic and reformed and allows its clergy considerable leeway in interpreting Anglican beliefs. It is also a rather arrogant organisation, claiming to have secured the truth of Christianity, forgetting that the vast majority of the world population who live outside of a small island just north of mainland Europe are not C of E, a hangover from the days of the Great British Empire, I suspect. The diversity of belief which forms the C of E results in some clergy being extreme Evangelicals, choosing not to wear clerical attire, ripping out their altars and furnishing their churches with screens, sound systems and music groups for the weekly "worship". At the other end of the spectrum there are those who are more catholic than your average Roman priest, choosing to use the term "Father" and to celebrate Mass rather than Holy Communion. Between these two extremes are a myriad of shades, each with its own unique descriptive term, and yet all Anglican.

Oxford too is a strange place and my choice of Theological College was no easy task. Oxford covers the shades of Anglicanism with three colleges. St Stephen's House (also known as Staggers) is situated off the Cowley road, and boasts more Roman Catholic Bishops from its Alumni than any other Anglican college! It is the bastion of high Anglo Catholicism. In the middle is Cuddesdon; nestled in the countryside a few miles out of Oxford it is renowned for being a place of liberalism. At the other extreme is Wycliffe Hall, an Evangelical College situated on the Banbury road, and when I was there the only college to be a Permanent Private Hall of the University. When I told my DDO (Diocesan Director of Ordinands – the bloke assigned to assist us through the Ordination process) that I wanted to go to Wycliffe, his mouth dropped, "You're not a Wycliffe man, Cuddesdon is the place for

you". No, I certainly wasn't a Wycliffe man, my theology was both high, in so far as ceremony and practice was concerned, and at the same time increasingly more liberal, a throwback to the days when I first came across the vicar who helped me into Reader Ministry. Wycliffe's liturgical practice was extremely low and theology was extremely conservative. True, there

were other factors at play that suited the family, I realised that Wycliffe would allow me to live off site, thus enabling me to be myself rather than live in a goldfish bowl. It was not this feature that I put to the DDO, but somehow I convinced him and this increasingly liberal Christian who enjoyed high and ornate liturgies applied, was accepted and began his studies in a conservative low liturgical college. It was to be a valuable experience.

My Bishop said that he had heard me loud and clear when he interviewed me in relation to where I would serve as a Curate. A Curate is best described as some doing "on the job training". It is the position held after Ordination in the Church of England, under the watchful eye of a senior and experienced priest. I was determined, having been to Wycliffe that I wasn't going to go to an Evangelical parish, and had filled in the application form in such a way that it was almost anti evangelicals! The Bishop could not have made a better recommendation.

It was suggested that I look at a Parish in South Northamptonshire, cared for by a priest who had gone to Staggers but was certainly not catholic, rather a healthy mix of Anglicanism. That was perhaps my state and so I went to visit him and it was decided that we could work together.

I will always be grateful to the vicar of that parish, Fr. Nicholas, he taught me more than I will ever know and his gentle guidance still informs much of what I do. It was no easy ride though (for him anyway). I was a bit of a maverick from day one, pushing boundaries, breaking rules and building up, although without intending to do so, quite a fan club from both within the church and the wider community.

My Bishop was rather niggled that during my time at University I had not experienced any time in chaplaincy (i.e. in a hospital or prison) and made it clear that I was to spend a day each week working in this area. It was arranged that I should become part of the local general hospital chaplaincy team and I reluctantly agreed. I don't remember the conversation, but apparently I arrived in the Chaplain's office at the local hospital to the fanfare, "Hello, I'm Christopher, I don't really want to be here, but hey ho!" It was to transform my Ministry, and bring my own faith structure to its knees.

Fr. Nicholas had already begun moulding me into a highly disciplined Priest, the Hospital Chaplain sought to undo all of this with what she called "the theology of being". In the Parish I was always "doing", visiting, ministering, listening, praying etc. There was a right way and a wrong way, and there were reasons for this as I was so thoroughly taught. My day began with Morning Prayer, rhythmic, methodical, deep, one half our slot at the start and end of each day when NOTHING got in the way. There was an ebb and flow to it, rather like the sea. The Hospital Chaplain turned all of this on its head, there was no right way, no wrong way, no reasons either way. Morning prayer at the chapel was what we could snatch, it followed no set pattern, and the bleep could go off at

Reg. in England No. 1413450

H&M are happy to exchange or refund any unsuitable garments within 28 days, provided they are in a resalable condition and a valid receipt is presented.

We regret that for reasons of hygiene we are unable to refund or exchange pierced earrings and cosmetic products.

This does not affect your statutory rights.

H&M

H & M HENNES & MAURITZ UK LIMITED.
1st Floor
25 Argyll Street
London W1F 7TS
Reg. in England No. 1413450

H&M are happy to exchange or refund any unsuitable garments within 28 days, provided they are in a resalable condition and a valid receipt is presented.

We regret that for reasons of hygiene we are unable to refund or exchange pierced earrings and cosmetic products.

This does not affect your statutory rights.

H&M

H & M HENNES & MAURITZ UK LIMITED.
1st Floor
25 Argyll Street
London W1F 7TS
Reg. in England No. 1413450

243070692

Salesman: T39185 Store: 00780 No: 3102
Date: 19/09/17 Time: 16:20

Jersey Tailor
05161G0 9.99

Total 9.99

*** THANK YOU FOR SHOPPING ***

any moment. The whole "job" was prayer. My role was just to be there, to be there for anyone and everyone no matter what their belief system, or lack of. It was a powerful tug between one way of Ministering and another, and yet the tugging opened doors. I could have easily settled into a quasi monastic way of Ministering, each day punctuated by Morning and Evening Prayer, saying Mass at various times, and thus "doing" becoming the focal point, the foundation stone for my work. "Being" meant that I felt a strong draw to be out there, in the community, in a similar way to my hospital role, just being there for everyone, talking, laughing, crying, smiling, just , well being.

In my second and third year I had the opportunity to set up a Multi-faith chaplaincy service within a secure Mental Health setting. I knew nothing about mental health, and very little about other faiths. As always, faced with a problem I found a way to solve it and so read for a Diploma, firstly in Psychiatric studies and secondly in Psychology, whilst at the same time trying to visit as many similar institutions as I could to look at how chaplaincy services were structured and how the multi faith interplay worked in practice.

My fairly limited understanding of multi faith working suggested to me that multi faith had its boundaries, Christianity, Islam, Hinduism, Buddhism and Judaism were all part of the set up. This cosy view was blown out of the water I was having lunch in another Mental Health institution and a lady, all dressed in black, was introduced to me. She was the Wicca chaplain. Asked afterwards by the Anglican Chaplain how my day was going I said that the lady I had been introduced to was "a bit outside my comfort zones". I explained that she seemed very nice, but Wicca? "Welcome to Multi faith Chaplaincy," was his reply.

One enduring memory was how stark multi faith rooms were. They were generally light rooms with white washed walls, but with no pictures, symbols etc., this, I was told was so as not to cause offence. I returned to the hospital I was working with, armed with ideas and experiences and sat down with a group of patients and staff to have a brainstorming session. It was decided that we SHOULD have a decorated room, with pictures and symbols but that in being sensitive we should look at something universal. After much discussion we came up with a scene depicting a rainbow, amongst other things, and a table with a ring of candles, reminding us clearly of the universal theme of the power of light over darkness...it took me right back to my pre confirmation viewing of Star Wars 30 years before! I absolutely loved my work in that hospital. I was there facilitating pastoral and spiritual care to ALL without exception. One minute I was a Roman Catholic Priest, the next a Pentecostal Minister, then a Vicar, then an Imam, or even just a human being. Of course part of my brief was to facilitate the provision of faith specific care, but this was not always immediate and so I had to adapt, learn and give as needed. The white collar around my neck was a powerful symbol, and I learned that most profoundly here. It took a lot of work to gain respect and confidence from patients and staff, but once that barrier had been crossed the work took off and blossomed. In the background I enjoyed Parish life, but the constant round of school assemblies, meetings, Eucharist's, pastoral care of those who were of the Christian faith only became a grind and I realised that my calling was not to Parish Ministry with its focus predominately on selling and maintaining one dogma, but rather being there for all and getting my hands dirty, metaphorically speaking, at the coal face of life.

Eventually, the time for me to consider my next move. Gone are the days when the Bishop assigns a priest to a new job, like the rest of the world the Church has become a place of completing job applications and of trying to sell oneself in interview. I did not want to enter Parish Ministry. I would have been quite happy to have stayed as Fr. Nicholas's Curate in perpetuity, in a community chaplaincy role – he could do all the "churchy" stuff and I
would do all the visiting, pastoral care etc etc, but the church doesn't work like that. Privately, I wanted to stay in Chaplaincy, particularly in Mental Health Chaplaincy, as I felt that those in an acute setting valued the chaplain perhaps more than in any other setting I had been involved in. "You are the only one who is not checking up on us and taking notes" one patient said, and this had always stuck with me. Sadly my domestic circumstances were such that I had to take into account other factors and there was considerable pressure to go into Parish

ministry. I decided that if that were the case I would need a fairly open minded and liberal Parish that would accept my style of doing things. I had also decided that I was no longer able to "play" at being a Priest. There was still a part of me that felt compelled to conform, to be "what they expected to be" and I decided that I wasn't going to do this anymore, so I reluctantly applied for a group of Parishes, and was invited for interview.

The Parishes were absolutely not my cup of tea. The former Incumbent had been a conservative Evangelical, and in Anglican terms the set up was fairly Low Church. I set great store in beautiful, if not too over fussy liturgies, beautiful traditional music, but with a bit of a down to earth, contemporary and liberal approach thrown in. The former Incumbent had an issue with raffles, so no raffle tickets at the church fête – I would have to change that!

In every conceivable way it just wasn't me.

In April 2007, I got in the car, wearing my new black clerical shirt together with the "so white you must have just been ordained" collar that came with it, my new black suit, shoes (and even black underpants) and set off for the interview day. I knew that I would court controversy from the moment I arrived. Black, all Black in Anglican circles is generally seen as a statement, "I am a Catholic!". I knew from the pictures that my predecessor never wore black. The Archdeacon for using the term "Father" in my title had already ticked me off. I did point out that I hadn't been accepted for the post and that this was my existing title, but he wasn't impressed. The Interview day was as I had expected, I was introduced to lots of smiling people, who wanted to know lots of things about me. They filled me with tea and fed me, along with the other candidates, before the interview itself.

The interview was in two parts, two panels with various gruelling questions. My first interview included one of the patrons (an organisation or person whose job it is to select new incumbents and who often are charged with ensuring that certain traditions or theologies are met). The Patron represented an Organisation called the Church Society, a very conservative, evangelical and powerful group. I took an instant dislike to the man. Within seconds of entering the room, after having being introduced to all present I became aware that the Patron's body language spoke of instant disapproval. This in turn flicked that rebellious switch within me and I goaded him with every answer to the other interviewers. I managed somehow to bring into every answer which were gracefully and articulately framed something which I knew would light his fuse, and the plan worked, when it was his turn he went for me like a raging bull.

Instead of backtracking or justifying my liberal position with eloquent arguments, or even trying to find middle ground I answered every question in a way which I knew would enrage him a little further. I had no truck for conservative views and was taking no prisoners, neither was her. I had , for the first time in my life stood up to narrow minded bigoted views and it felt good The Bishop asked the final questions and led me out for a cup of tea. I turned to the Bishop and said" I'm going home now." He smiled, put his hand on my shoulder and said "don't worry about it". In that moment alone, drinking my tea I decided that I would approach the next interview completely differently. No eloquent replies to questions, no telling them what they want to hear, no trying to make a statement. I was just going to be myself.

"Now, Christopher, could you tell us what you understand by the Doctrine of Penal Substitution?", " Um, gosh, that was the day I dozed off in lectures, well, it's a concept that God sent his own son to die for us wicked sinners.
All a load of rubbish really, that's if you believe in a Loving God."

"Christopher, what's your take on raffles", " Love them, best thing about church fêtes, why, do you have any to sell, what's the first prize?"

I was thanked for my time, got into the car and drove the 140 miles home. A couple of hours later I leaned on a lamp post outside the Chinese on my mobile 'phone. "It's complicated, but you've' got the job !" the Bishop announced. I was relieved , I can't say I was happy with the news, but relieved that I didn't have to go through the process again, the complications of other factors were resolved and at least I had a job to go to. I wandered into the Chinese to get a few sweet and sour chicken balls and some fried rice, and whilst they prepared the meal I popped over to the local "offi" to get a couple of bottles of wine. It was rumoured that the wine was in celebration, but privately it was in commiseration.

Something good was to become of that day. I had stood up to narrow minded views, I had for the first time in years just been myself (and apparently that's what swung it for me), but something even better happened. I had a meeting which years later was to change my life. Over lunch a well-dressed young lady appeared in front of me. She was part of the constant stream of people wanting to say "hello" she introduced herself to me, with a wide smile and sparkling eyes and advised me that she was a member of the PCC (The Church Council). "Oh, I don't do PCC's, I prefer to just light blue touch paper and retire" was my response.

This Angel in disguise was one day to be my wife.

So, I packed up my worldly goods, and headed off to my new role, with a bit of a pay rise thrown in.

The Church of England is not immune to bullshit. Fr Nicholas had done a good job in his usual wise way of reading in-between the lines that this was a problem parish. However, it wasn't until I was moved in and duly Installed that the reality became clear and was spelled out to me. A very tiny but powerful core of church members ruled the roost. This included two members of my team, one retired Bishop and a Reader. My task was to get in there and sort the ethos out. Probably that's why they wanted a maverick approach. I made my presence known from day one and with full support of my Bishop began the process of change.

I preached inclusivity and Love from the pulpit, gently but firmly denouncing religious conservatism and bigotry and even throwing in a few quotes from Monty Python's Life of Brian for good measure. It had the Marmite effect, my sermons were either loved or hated. Fortunately it was only a small core that fell into the latter camp. The most important medium for change was the parish magazine whose readership extended well beyond the church doors, and I gradually ratcheted up my message. The editor of the magazine was not pleased. Although not a stooge of the Church Society he might as well have been and he attempted to block some of my "Rectors Messages" , on the grounds that they were unscriptural. We had a conversation along the lines of "look you may not agree with my take on things, but I am the Rector, therefore I am allowed to write in a way I feel fit", he wouldn't budge. So, I sent him an email. "Dear....... Just to let you know , in the next couple of issues of the magazine I want to include major articles on sticky subjects. Next month I am going to be writing about Multi Faith issues, helping people to see what we have in common and to be more respectful , and even consider working with other faith groups. The following months I am going to tackle the thorny issue of sexuality and dispel some of the crazy ideas that God condemns homosexuals" The time gap between the sending of the email and his sitting in my study has to be a world record, especially as his house was a mile away. He duly resigned on the spot, told me I had given my soul to Satan and the parish magazine became a place of growth and debate once more. I never did write those articles.

The church hierarchy told me I was doing a great job, they were pleased with reports coming back to them and despite a wobbly first six months, I had nothing to worry about. I was, however, finding that so much of my time was taken up by church politics, explaining why I never went to or hosted Bible study groups. I was going to meeting after meeting after meeting. It was draining me.

When I was a Curate, I had to attend what we called potty training once a month. Fairly early on we had a talk by a former Archdeacon who talked about being more accommodating during weddings, baptisms and funerals when we were facilitating these for non-churchgoers. During the course of discussion a name arose which seemed to cause some disapproval from those in the know, with a splattering of intense approval by others. The name was Jonathan Blake.

Jonathan left the Church of England in the 1990's in order, initially, to work independently of any denomination and to offer a ministry of Unconditional Love to All without exception. He was no longer bound by books and would create beautiful, bespoke liturgies to match the person's needs and the occasion. Of particular interest to me was his approach to funerals. I still had some regret at having had to leave the funeral trade to be Ordained and harboured thoughts of returning at some stage, somehow combining the Priesthood with Funeral work. Jonathan could create a service for the family concerned. He didn't have to wear robes, or use hymns if the family didn't want him to, he could make the service absolutely special and unique.

I LIKED that approach and so looked him up. By now he was an Archbishop of a church established to mirror his vision. I felt a tingle.........it was everything I felt I was called to do, minister with no walls, boundaries or agenda, except love. Minister to ALL, regardless of gender, sexuality, faith or even no faith, just be there for people , be in the world as a Priest rather than in this infuriating bubble of institutionalised religion. I wanted to jump, and jump now, but the time wasn't right, so I watched his Ministry from afar.

A couple of years into my new job, things began to crumble. I was a square peg in a round hole. In the streets, shops, pubs, amongst the general population all that I did was valued and loved, but within the small hard core of church members the pressure began to build. In the mean time things came to a head at home and I entered into what would turn out to be a very acrimonious and messy divorce. With no children at home, they had all grown up, no-one to consult about where I should be ministering it was just me, God and the big wide world. For the first time in my life I had choice, for the first time I was free to be me. Due to complications surrounding my divorce I was asked to take a year away from ministry. It was a painful request to answer in the affirmative and I initially resisted doing so, but was persuaded that it was the right thing. I duly packed up all my goods and chattels once again and moved to a much smaller house in a completely new area. For the first time in years I was , to all intents and purposes a layperson again. No one called me "vicar", I didn't wear a clerical collar, and I felt utterly devoid of my vocation and calling , as if I had been thrust to one side and left to die. Of course it was only for a year, and although the road back would not be instantaneous, beginning perhaps with something part time, eventually I would be back to where I was before. This was no consolation.

Did I really want to go back to being a Parish priest? Did I really want to work within the walls of the Church of England. I went back time and time again to Jonathan website , story, and the email correspondence and conversations we had been having now for a couple of years and had to ask myself a life changing question. Should I join him?

The small hard core of my former parish had continued be cause problems for me even when I had left. They were joined now by a local Archdeacon who, knowing very little of the situation had formed an opinion and displayed an attitude that was as remote from Christianity as it could ever be. I saw a very different side to the Church of England, a side that is contradictory to all they profess to stand for. Coupled to this was the emotional pull of letters coming through the door from parishioners who had written to the Bishop to ask for me to come back, and regular calls of support. The action taken by the church authorities perhaps caused those in authority more damage that they will ever realise. Certainly conversations I have had with former parishioners from that time have indicated this. Even now ordinary parishioners who tell me they want me back apparently speak me of with great affection.

I felt that it was unwise to join Jonathan until my year out was over – I didn't want anyone to think or suggest that I had been pushed and wanted it to be abundantly clear that this was my decision based on considerable thought and prayer. In the July of 2011, I went to see Jonathan with my decision. I was leaving the Church of England.

FREEDOM ! New Horizons and walls coming down.

My decision to leave the Church of England was met with a mixed response.

To some (the "Safe Set") their concerns were about going it alone, "what about supporting yourself, pension, housing etc?". I had none of these at the time supplied by the Church and so none of them were an issue except that I suppose what it meant was that they were never going to be a safety net again. There were other comments made about the "wackiness" of the Open Episcopal Church , and Jonathan's own Ministry. I responded by saying that anyone can read into articles found on the Internet, but unless you have met the people involved you can't really offer an informed opinion. Those closest to me, however, were thrilled, it was an opportunity to follow a calling that had grown within me, to be the Priest that God wanted me to be without the constraints of the organisation of the C of E.

There were some legalities than needed to be settled, it was important to sever ties with the Church of England completely and this involved "Relinquishing" my right to exercise my exercise my Ministry within the Church of England. Not everyone chooses to do this, a great many former Anglican's are still legally Anglican Priests, but I wanted to sever ties absolutely. This was important as it meant that the C of E had no further legal or moral hold over me. This took some time to go through the legal process, but once done I was free. I wrote confirming my desire to be relinquished to my Bishop as the last stage of the process.

I had a fairly cordial reply from my Anglican Bishop who wished me well for the future, which was nice !

Now, dear reader, a bit of church politics here for you to get your head around, are you sitting comfortably ? All explanations are in brackets !

The Open Episcopal Church is a direct descendant of the See of Utrecht (an area on the continent which in medieval times was uniquely given the powers to do all sorts of things including Ordaining Bishops without asking the Pope first). As such it is an Old Catholic Jurisdiction (too long to explain, if you are interested there is always Google !).

In Church terms there is a question in these jurisdictions (Catholic jurisdictions) about the validity of Orders of those within the Anglican Church. (A pope in the 19th Century declared that all Anglican (Church of England etc) Ordinations were invalid, and thus clergy in the Church of England are seen as nothing more than lay people). In practice, the whole debate is utter nonsense, but in order to ensure that everyone in the OEC had the same Lineage (i.e. Bob Ordained Fred, who Ordained Reg, who Ordained Steve.....right back to the time of the Apostles) everyone joining the OEC from the Church of

England has to be Ordained Sub Conditione (Latin for "we are not sure if you have been Ordained properly so we will do it again just in case).

A friend at the time said to me "Oh , you've got to go through it all again!" I was actually quite excited about the prospect, it marked a watershed, it was a wonderful way of defining my new Ministry, AND as the OEC allows all clergy to create a Liturgy that reflects their theology and Ministry (save the Ordination bits which are fixed) it meant that I could at least have considerable choice about what happened. So I began work on the service. It was beautiful. It was long, very long, almost 3 hours, and I chose to stick to a traditional Catholic Rite with a huge amount of ceremony involved. During the service I had the wonderful privilege of Confirming Natasha into the catholic faith. It all went well, and I was buzzing. The venue chosen for the service was that Knights Chamber at the town hall in Kings Lynn, directly opposite a very large Anglican Church. After the service, Archbishop Jonathan, a dear friend who acted as server/deacon and I went to disrobe in a room directly facing the Anglican Church. Jonathan left quickly to go and see the congregation of family and friends. I grinned at my friend, and decided upon one final act of defiance, a Father Ted moment – I jumped up and down with two fingers in the air smiling at the Anglican Church. All very silly, very childish but nonetheless very cathartic indeed !

I had crossed the Tiber !

Looking back now, my spirituality, belief system, theology etc could clearly be defined as liberal catholic. I was still very much an Anglican , but working outside of the walls of Anglicanism, on the fringes. A daily Mass was important , and I would of course ensure that I robed, fully to celebrate at our home altar. So too was fixed liturgical Morning and Evening Prayer. I was just an Ex Anglican Priest, now in Catholic Orders working within a
breakaway church. I remember sitting on our sofa after the Ordination Service, which took place in December 2011. I turned to Natasha and asked " what now?". In her usual deep and intuitive way, her look said more thanher words, "you just need to get out there and be you !"

Getting out there was easier said than done. The local churches wanted nothing to do with me when I suggested that I might join "Churches together". The response was that I "neither have a building nor a congregation thus you cannot be a part of us". My response went into some paragraphs pointing out the theology of "church" being nothing to do with a building and listing the numbers of those I was ministering to by way of taking services each week – it didn't make any difference , the answer was "No".

It is only when we stand back, and look , when we really look that we see reality. For years I had been part of a church that said that it was loving, embracing and forgiving. As I began to view it from the outside I saw a distinct lack of love, a culture of exclusivity and ecclesial arrogance devoid of forgiveness. As I began to work with the "ordinary" folks in the world I was touched by their common stories, "the vicar refused to baptise my child, conduct our marriage, didn't even mention my granddad's name at the funeral, and he was late. I used to go to church but it was very cliquey, I didn't feel welcomed, or, I was pounced upon and then felt obliged to join all sorts of groups, but I was still the outsider. We wanted the Baptist Minister to take Mum's funeral but in the village church, the vicar wouldn't let us. My fiancé had been married twice, and we know it's right this time, but the vicar said no. I was a clergyman many years ago, I foolishly had a fling with a parishioner for which I was defrocked. They still won't entertain any possibility of my being involved in church life in any way". These are just some of the very many examples I have come across in my Ministry. The most disturbing is what I would clearly define as spiritual abuse.

Spiritual Abuse is considered to be rare, linked with fringe and extreme cults. No, actually Spiritual Abuse goes on in towns and villages across the country, in cosy churches and chapels people are being abused , not just by their clergy but by other church members. For example, there is nothing whatsoever to stop a Minister from ascending the pulpit and denouncing the "sin" of homosexuality, formulating an argument that it will result in hell, the minister may even know that Mrs Jones in the back pew has been living with her "sister" for many years, but , no , it's OK to condemn , the Bible says so. Now, if you were to take the same line outside of the pulpit, say on the bus stand up and call the gay couple snuggled at the back sinners who are going to hell, you may find yourself arrested. It's OK though to do it in church. This is just one of myriad examples. The bottom line is that whenever a religious institution or its people entice others in with promises of love, forgiveness and hope, and then temper this promise with "but of course if you do this or that......you're going to be going to be going to hell, or more subtlety, you need forgiveness, there is abuse and the abuse is rife. I realised that I too had been a perpetrator of Spiritual Abuse every week, often more than once a week ….......I had said, publicly proclaimed time and time again ….

"YE that do truly and earnestly repent you of your sins, and are in love and charity with your neighbours, and intend to lead a new life, following the commandments of God, and walking from henceforth in his holy ways:
Draw near with faith, and take this holy Sacrament to your comfort; and make your humble confession to Almighty God, meekly kneeling upon your knees."

Or in other words....

Those of you who are determined to turn away from all that you do that is wrong, that is contrary to the teachings I expound from the Bible, and all those myriad things we do every day that the church calls "sin" and IF you have made it up with everyone you have pissed off, not just this week, but throughout your whole life and love everyone, really truly love everyone, you who follow God's commandments to THE LETTER, which means not even thinking things contrary to them and from this moment onwards are committed to and promise to be pure and Holy at all times. Then, and only then, we will let you share in the bread and wine of Communion, but before you do so, even though you have genuinely committed yourself to these things, you need to confess your sins, just like you did, yesterday, last week or whenever you came last time, and YOU NEED TO DO IT ON YOUR KNEES, thereby begging God for mercy.

Once those miserable worthless sinners had done ALL this, and confessed their sins I would dispense Absolution – WHAT ON EARTH WAS I THINKING??????

As time went on and I worked in the world, away from organised and carefully marketed religion I saw more and more the rot within. I saw how it abuses, constrains, and in complete contrast to its claims entraps and imprisons rather than brings about hope. This strengthened my faith, it didn't diminish it at all. The people I was working with were looking for love, reassurance and guidance. They wanted to grow, experience , be free, they didn't want to be abused by the negativity found in so much religious teaching . They wanted to learn about God. I was being asked to help.

Throughout the early days of my new Ministry I remained an ultra liberal Anglican, at heart anyway. I tweaked liturgies to be more "user friendly" and less "churchy" , patting myself on the back that I could do it !

During one funeral service in early 2012 , I remember glancing around the congregation during the words of the Committal. I had tweaked them a bit, but in reality they were fairly standard Church of England words. I sensed a feeling of numbness, of vacantness, of detachment. I thought deeply about this afterwards and realised that it was not necessarily what was happening at that time, namely the curtains were closing at the crematorium, but rather that my words meant nothing to the ordinary person out there. The ordinary person out there in the ordinary real world whose loved one I was saying farewell to. My words were simply background noise as they sought to make sense of that final moment in their own words. "he will transform our frail bodies that they may be like unto his glorious bodies" meant little or nothing. So, I sat in front of my computer and played with some different words , words that were loving, inclusive, meaningful, spiritual, words that instead of forming a background noise would instead take the hand of all present and walk with them at this poignant moment. After a couple of weeks of playing around I came up with a number of possibilities and with a funeral in the diary decided to give it a go.

Funeral ministry is a strange and sensitive subject where certain things should not be measured. The question of "did I get it right" is of course in a way important, but right can involve navel gazing, perhaps the question is made up of a number of factors involving connectedness, empathy, sympathy, etc. As these questions , important ones when dealing with the bereaved, buzzed around my head following the funeral I happened to bump into a relative of the person who had passed away a few days later, "Oh, I have to tell you we were so pleased, the words you said as the curtains closed were so moving and the bit about Reg being safe in the arms of God has meant so much to us". I have learned over the years to accept praise when given, not that I ever expect it, and my desire here was to create something for the bereaved, not for myself, and in any case anything that is created needs to be fluid , but it was the evidence I needed that my hunch was right and from that moment until now, unless specifically requested, I have never used a "standard" service.

This process of discernment , and the daily work began to change me. It challenged my theology. My world view, as Christian, was seen against the background of Christian teaching as I had received it. I considered myself a "mature" Christian, I had some 5 years academic study under my belt, I was able to discern, argue and evangelise, I had a deep prayer life. It then hit me one day that Christian maturity is not about knowing our way around the Bible, the doctrines of the Church or our prayer life, its rather about putting it into practice, removing the trappings of what goes on within church and going out. Christian maturity is about LIVING the Gospel of unconditional Love, rather than spouting it !

The walls, already cracked and broken in places began to crumble. When they started there was nothing stopping them.

One of my hobbies is Morris Dancing. I needed something to do which was completely different to everything else, something fun, enjoyable, but challenging as well. I have never been a dancer, two left feet and no rhythm, but I thought I would give it a go and was hooked after the first session. I am still at a fairly early stage, still lots to learn, however , some 10 months in I am beginning to notice something interesting. When I first took up this hobby, I was shown how to move my feet, what to do with my hands and where to move my whole body to. All this has to be done in synchronicity with the other dancers. There's a lot to think about, and if you think it looks easy, it's not. Everything has to be done in harmony with the music that is playing. As time went on , during the weekly 2 hour rehearsals, difficult moves that required one brain controlling my legs and another controlling my hands became easier, once the legs and foot movements were mastered, I could forget about them and concentrate on the hands (or vice versa). Eventually , as each dance was cracked, it then became fun, especially when the time came to perform in public. Over the first summer I signed up for every single outing and danced the same dances over and over and over again. They became ingrained. But something else interesting happened. In "cracking" the dances I found that I went beyond the mechanics and learned to "feel" and experience the deeper side of the dances and the music. Morris dancing has become a spiritual experience, but it only became so when I learned to let go of the mechanics and enter into what I am doing in a deep way. This has had a knock on effect in other areas, particularly in relation to sounds and music, I no longer "hear" the wind in the trees , and "feel" its impact on my body, but I experience and harmonise with the wind, it is not a separate entity , outside of me, but I connect with it, wind is just one example. During my regular visits to the coast, I still find God, the ebb and flow of the waves continues to open a channel of communication, which is two way. I now find myself in synchronicity with the sea, part of it, in harmony with it. It is no longer a place where I go to BE with God, the waves exist within my very being, God is there too in a way I have never experienced before.

I share this insight as it in a way underpins much of what I have experienced in relation to the broken walls that I described a moment ago.

For years, my faith was , yes of course experiential, but within a context and a boundary. Rather like when I lived in Berlin as a child, although I was free with my parents to live, eat, breath and explore, only a few miles away was a huge wall, that marked not only the line between east and west, but it was a cultural divide as well. It set the parameters of my existence.

Christianity and only Christianity was my Berlin Wall for years. I knew a little of what lay outside, or at least what

I had been told lay outside, but had bought into the whole delusion that I was inside the correct place, the one and only place. Christianity was THE only one true expression of faith and spirituality. The bible was the very word of God, the Church was its human expression of it, and my task, at least as a Priest was to expound that Word, to dispense the Sacraments and to bring others into the fold. I had discovered something amazing, the one true religion – nothing else would do, everything else was flawed and all who had not bought into Christianity were doomed to hell.

During the last year of my Anglican Ministry, I was "on holiday" one Sunday and realised that I didn't have any milk. Unless I was prepared to put on a false beard , or drive 4 miles to the nearest town I ran the risk of being accosted or frowned upon by members of my flock heading to Church that morning. So I decided to wait until they were all in Church before venturing out to get some milk. As I rounded the corner and came into hearing distance of the church I heard the Organ thundering and the 90 or so people within singing away. It was one of those modern hymns that spoke of "MY God", MY Salvation" etc, rather than the more traditional hymns that tend to use collective words. As I walked towards the shop, I noticed the people NOT at Church, it was a bright sunny day, and people were walking dogs, chatting , smiling, laughing. These were all the people we considered to be unsaved, they didn't seem miserable, empty, devoid of depth or spirituality , all the things I had considered after years of brain washing that could be solved by going to Church, they were OK.

This had a profound effect on me, and I wanted to know what life meant to them.

FREEDOM !

After December 2011, I entered 2012 with a buzz, I could Minister to ALL in need, without the bureaucracy, dogmas and politics of the C of E. Having now also gone back, in a small way at least into the funeral trade, an area I felt most comfortable in, it followed that many of my contacts within that industry asked me to not only to work for them as a pall bearer but were excited too about my new absolute flexibility as a Minister and Priest.

Up until as recently as 25 years the Church of England basically had the monopoly on funerals. This was partly cultural, the vast majority of people would , on the death of a loved one state that their loved one was C of E coupled with an expectation that a standard C of E funeral was the "right thing to do". This was also to do with the attitude of the C of E. The Parochial system that exists to this day is such that a Priest has "cure of Souls" for each person in their parish(s) which in effect means that every person in England, regardless of belief or background is considered to be
under the care of the relevant Priest. In effect this meant that unless a family expressed a different denominational or religious allegiance the Funeral Director would automatically call the vicar, and the family would then be at his mercy – some are flexible, sensitive and understanding, others, even now, display a

level of arrogance that causes distress to families rather than helping them through the pain of grief. Over the last 25 years there has been a huge cultural shift towards funerals being more personal, and pitched at a level, in terms of religious content, that engages with the family. This has coincided with the rise in what are termed "Civil" funerals. A Civil funeral can combine religious and not religious material. Celebrants are generally not Ordained Ministers but are trained in the use of prayers and hymns. Indeed their training is far more comprehensive and varied that the training I received as an Anglican Priest ! I had one weeks training at university and 4 days of that was looking at the theology of death ! The Church of England no longer has the monopoly, even though it would like to.

I spoke to a funeral director friend of mine and explained that like a Civil Celebrant I now had absolute flexibility over the content and the style of a funeral service. Where a family were C of E, but not active members and wanted that to be acknowledged I could put together a service to reflect that but with personal material as well. He told me that so many families fitted into that category, and he would give me a go the next time a family came in who wanted something a little different. The very next day the phone rang and my Funeral Ministry took off in earnest.

In the last few years I have had the immense privilege of conducting over 500 funerals. Each and every one has been unique and different. I have taken everything from

completely non-religious funerals to Roman Catholic Rite services and everything in-between. I have combined belief systems, created prayers and poems, and have been asked to help families from humanist, catholic, Methodist, c of e , Wicca, spiritualist, Bahia, eclectic and Jewish backgrounds to name but a few. It is the most rewarding part of my Ministry because it fits beautifully with my work on the other side of the funeral fence. I care deeply about people, and want to create a service and
celebrate their loved one's life in a way which is meaningful and connects with them at every level.

One day, driving back from the Crematorium I received a telephone call from a local burial site. Someone was putting together a film with its focus on how to engage and be more innovative in Funeral Ministry. Staff in the chapel had observed a couple of funerals I had taken and had recommended me to star in the film ! Was I happy to do this? My answer was of course in the affirmative, I am very happy to share my approach with anyone who wants to put families first and so I was thanked and very quickly an exchange of emails took place. I realised early on that the people organising the film were of course the C of E, but just for old times' sake thought I would play along, inevitably they worked out that I was not one of them and so I was politely stood down.

About 6 months into my new Ministry, I had a moment of self doubt – I remember thinking one morning, "is this what I have given up all that I had in the C of E for, to

spend 85% of my time as a funeral celebrant with a dog collar on?". That momentary question said more about the walled institution that I was formally a part of and who had schooled me in a Theology and a set of dogmas than it did about me. I remembered that funerals in the C of E were rarely a big thing, all part of a day's work, and also that many clergy, not including myself, found them to be rather a chore unless of course it was an important parishioner that had passed away. Other things like Evangelism, Dispensing the Sacraments , building a larger Church
Community etc were of far more importance than the tedious chore of burying the dead. That was the mindset that I was working with, things were now different. I was BEING a Priest at a deeply profound level. I would argue at THE most deepest level. A Priest can say Mass, dispense Absolution, expound the Scriptures, and everything else a Priest is called to do , and in all these things would claim to stand in persona Christi (to be as

Jesus to others in that moment), and yet he or she is not actually being Jesus to others but rather being what the church, its tradition, its politics or its congregation THINKS Jesus should be. Dressing up in fine vestments, genuflecting before consecrated bread, plodding around the parish with a white collar that only the clergy wear actually has little, indeed nothing to do with being as Jesus to others. It is rather about being the CHURCH to others and the church is a dying institution.

One of the most poignant illustrations of this happened in early 2013 when I had two funerals, at different crematoria, but timing was such that I had rather a tight schedule. The first funeral was a non-religious one, a beautiful and meaningful service celebrating the life of the person who had passed away through a selection of music, readings and a time to reflect. Naturally I conducted the funeral in my suit and tie. After the funeral I popped into the vestry where a middle aged Anglican Priest sat ready to take the funeral after me, I said "hello" and popped into the gents only to emerge in clerical attire (black shirt and white collar) . The look said it all. "Oh, I'm multi tasking today", I said, " I have just conducted the most beautifully put together non-religious funeral and am now hot footing it to another crematorium to take a Church of England style service." She shook her head and asked how I could do such a thing, as a Priest my calling was to bring others to God , particularly at a time when they had lost a loved one. How could I take a service devoid of any religious content. I replied , " whether it is religious, spiritual or humanist, I am still being as Jesus to the family. I am doing what he did, speaking in a language that engages with them compassionately . If that language is devoid of religion, it doesn't matter it is being there that matters." She just didn't get it, I had to cut the conversation short, politely and speed off the 45 miles to my next service. This interaction had a deep effect upon me, it confirmed what I already knew , namely that funeral ministry is NOT second rate, or "just all I now do because I can't do anything else" but that it is a wonderful, privileged, deep Ministry which had only become so because I was able to offer flexibility.

It's not just my reflecting upon what I do that has had a deep affect on me, but also the interaction of Ministry to others. There is a wrongly help assumption that clergy only Minister TO others. It is not just an assumption held in society but within the ranks of the clergy themselves. When I was at University we were taught a technique known in the trade as "theological reflection" . Theological reflection is a powerful reminder that in each and every interaction we are also Ministered TO, it is a two way process, and
as a result of each interaction if we keep an open mind, we grow. I have never had a problem with this, but have met so many clergy who do. They have reached the summit of their faith understanding , sometimes many years before even going through the Ordination process and their interactions are clouded by an arsenal of prejudices and implacability. I want to grow, I want to be open to God I want to experience that presence. I have done the "boxing God in" thing – whenever I have done that, everything outside is naturally devoid of God, but of course as I have matured and as I have been Ministered to, I have seen God in too many places to be able to pin him down to one narrow faith expression. In my interactions with others, with bereaved families and in other areas of my Ministry I have met the most beautiful people, loving , kind, caring, sure in their beliefs and faith. Almost none of them attend any form of organised religious gathering. Many of them have thought things through, they are not inarticulate,

misguided or lost, they are living their faith, their way bringing love and joy into the lives of those who they meet. I have experienced these people in the dark places of this world, and in the light. I have met the most wonderful atheists who , although certain that there is nothing beyond what we see and experience, no divine or spiritual powers, they display and live out a life which is beyond simply "moral" and in so many cases show a level of maturity and love that is devoid from the average churchgoer.

I have learned so much from Ministering away from organised religion , at the coal face in the real world away from a head and diary filled with "church" things. It has opened my eyes and torn down those walls. None of this has led me to question my faith, or indeed my vocation, it has instead enriched both in ways that I could not have imagined even five years ago. My "church" is no longer a building, it is the world in which I live. My mission is no longer to bring people to Jesus, but to try in some small way to be like him, to share love and compassion unconditionally. My belief system is no longer regulated by an institution that claims the monopoly on faith and asserts that it is the only way, I am free to explore the richness of philosophies, religions and how human beings connect with life. I am no longer constrained by one way, the right way, the only way, but instead , arrayed before my very eyes are as many ways as there are grains of sand on the sea shore. This , of course may sound to some that it's all about me, "I've seen the light", it's actually not about me at all, it's about how I can fulfil my calling, a calling I did not choose , to be for others. Not to be for a small sector of society, for only those who wear the badge of a particular faith group, but to be for all, without exception.

Some friends of mine keep chickens. They breed them on a small scale and have a number of beautiful pure breeds , with the most gorgeous eggs! A few years ago they decided to re home some battery chickens. The three most scraggy , forlorn looking hens arrived, almost blinking in the bright sunshine. These hens had been born for one purpose, to produce eggs. Their ultimate fate was for their wings and legs to end up as someone's Friday evening takeaway and the rest of them in a frozen pie or tin of dog food. What a life! These three birds had taken their first steps without the warmth and love of a mother figure, and, when the time came they were housed in a tiny cage , never seeing the light of day, fed, watered, kept warm until such time as their egg production began to diminish. Their whole existence was conditioned, artificial, they were devoid of the opportunity to make normal responses to normal situations, they were just a means to our insatiable greed.

There they were , blinking in the sun light, and for the first time, they began to scratch about, ruffle their feathers and flap their wings. One was a bit more adventurous than the others and began to have a good look around their spacious environment. She sat down for a while , making some intermittent cooing noises, and then with great gusto she stood up to reveal her newly laid egg. She strutted around clucking with satisfaction, almost saying "thank you". I observed these hens over time and noted that not only did they settle in almost immediately but like all living things they had their own individual personalities.

I have often reflected on these three hens and have drawn comparisons between religion and battery farming. As Christians, we are commanded to love, it is up there, right at the top, we thus try to love because we have been told to, conditioned to (with of course the threat of damnation if we don't). Like the battery hen our world is completely artificial, conditioned by a view , not created by God, but created by those who tell us what to believe. They suggest that religion brings freedom, I suggest otherwise. We are told God loves us as we are, and then constantly reminded of our utter sinfulness. Religion is full of contradictions. Love your neighbour, but condemn gays, forgive your enemies, but you are blessed when you dash the heads of their little ones against the rocks. Of course , challenge anyone with a Bible in their hand on these things and you are in for a big fight — it is the very word of God, God wrote it, word for word and of course in our own native tongue. The truth of course is very different and what we have is simply a collection of writings from antiquity of a number of genres that were put together because they, in total , represented the religious interpretation that the church wanted us to adhere to. Why are there so many books excluded from the Bible? It's not because they necessarily have lesser value, but rather because they raise awkward questions that do not conform to the caged religion that we have created. The Bible is a beautiful collection of writings with profound insights that speak to us in a myriad of ways about the nature of life, death, and of God. These writings also talk of a jealous God, an angry God, a wrathful God a God who allows and encourages genocide, murder, rape, child abuse and much much more.

Challenge a Bible wielding Christian and they will have a text to throw at you to justify anything. They delude themselves that they are free, when in fact they are caged, cutting themselves off from the real beauty and religion of love that this world has to offer, that God has given and continues to give us.

Love, the central message of Jesus, is not commanded, taught or conditional.
Love is experiential, natural, and without limits. It is a human response to God TO love, it can never be love when we simply follow a commandment.

In the summer of 2011, our beautiful little daughter, Bronwen Maria was born. She came into this world surrounded by so much love at home, but due to some complications Natasha had to be taken to the local hospital, leaving me, a Dad again, holding this little bundle who was occasionally opening just one eye and staring somewhat vacantly at the strange new world around her. I chatted to her, told her about her Mummy and Daddy, her siblings, her wider family, told her where she lived and what a wonderful life she was going to have. I held her in my arms for some 90 minutes until Natasha was able to do so once again. That was a deeply spiritual experience, a moment I will never forget on so many levels. As I drove home from the hospital after all was well to grab a couple of hours sleep, I prayed. I thanked God for our little angel. I thanked God for a safe entry into the world, and of course that Natasha was OK. I then began thinking about how beautiful the whole experience was, how perfect and beautiful Bronwen was. I thought also about what her life might be like, how things had changed in the 20 or so years since my grown up children had been born.

But as I lay in bed I thought about how utterly non nonsensical the Jewish/Christian belief is that wanted to say to me that Bronwen was born with a deep spiritual cancer, that of Original Sin. How ridiculous that we should ever even contemplate that she needed to be Baptised to be cleansed of that Sin. How can that tiny helpless baby , born out of love be anything other than a product of that love? How can she be sinful, corrupt, bad, damned to eternity in hell. This swam around my head and it became more an more an utterly ridiculous proposition to me. It was important to us that we marked her birth with Baptism, but Baptism in terms of a dedication to all that is good, to God, and a celebration of her birth, so that's what we did.

This experience continued to vex me, after all I was now outside of the battery cage of the Church of England, and indeed of most other denominations and religions. As time went on it became more and more unreasonable to believe in those central themes of the Christian church. That we are born in utter need of forgiveness, that we continue to sin and need forgiveness and that God sent his son to die so that we could be forgiven seemed more and more a view of God which was Satanic rather than the from God I was now experiencing , the God of Love. I have often helped people to understand matters of faith and belief by using analogies, probably because in my early days I too found that method helpful, I still do.

It hit me, it didn't just occur but hit me like a bolt from the blue. God, the Divine, whatever we want to call him/her is a sort of celestial parent. God has created us, and sustains us throughout our lives, in the minds of believers anyway. God is unfathomable (a wonderful tool of the church to again keep us true to their own teachings), and so any analogy only touches the surface (so we are told). So, Dad (God) brings to life EVERYTHING. Dad gives them all they need, but tells his children NOT to touch the fruit on a certain tree. They ignore Dad and have a bit of fruit (come on, we all know that forbidding children to do something has the effect of them being more determined to do it – been there, done that, got the t-shirt both as a child and as a parent). Dad goes spare (an understatement) , kicks them out and tells them that they are so bad that it's virtually impossible for them to have a relationship with him again. The story continues - cock up after cock up, of Dad throwing his dummy out of his pram time and time again. There are poems and stories of how one day Dad turns up with the goods, and how on other days he just leaves them to their own devices. Eventually Dad gets so sick of their behaviour (and of course the Bible tells us that what he did was out of so much love) that he sends his special son (who is actually God in disguise......no let's not complicate matters, let's just stick with Dad's number one goody goody son) and Dad then murders him, not only that he inflicts unimaginable suffering in the process.

Hum......crap springs to mind.

If this is all true, then one day I will stand corrected and , according to the teachings of the church be shown the error of my ways. I'm prepared to take that gamble. I am sure that this is where some readers will reach for their email account to tell me what a wicked sinner I am, OK, fine, you are entitled to your opinion. I have experienced God, in deep and profound ways, I have experienced God and experience God every day and at the most profound level God is experienced through and in love.

So, if God is Love, where does this story leave us?

It makes no sense, it confuses and condemns. Love plays no part in this traditional interpretation of what really happened. Am I thus tearing up the Bible? No on the contrary. I am seeing it in the light of one who is free. It wasn't God who condemned human beings, it wasn't God who killed his son, it was human beings, religious human beings, people who claimed to represent God, to stand for and live by God's principles and teachings. The very fact that God seemingly did nothing about it was more a display of how we are all loved in equal measure than trying to teach us a lesson. And that is the point, it's not that we are so utterly bad that God wants us to jump through hoops that we can never every jump through, it is that we are born so utterly good and perfect that God loves us unconditionally for who we are. God wants us to be ourselves, not a church/religious manufactured robot who smiles sweetly on a Sunday morning and then goes home to be something very different. God loves us as we are and , like the perfect parent wants us to be ourselves, to know we are loved and to be happy , happy with our lives and happy with ourselves. That is the key message of the Gospels, it is not the crucifixion and resurrection, it is the core every day interactions of Love.

As I have Ministered in the world and been ministered too, the beautiful people I meet every day, who claim no tangible religious affiliation, or in the case of those who do make such a claim do not attend a gathering of like minded people display one thing that I have noticed is lacking so often in religious circles, namely what you see is what you get ! They don't live double lives preaching one thing and practising another. They don't claim to be "saved" , which in itself suggests that others are not, they just live their lives, following what they feel is right, connects and makes some sense of it all, they are generally happy with their lives, happy with themselves. So often where there is unhappiness and pain, it is not an absence of God, but rather a pressure to be something other than what we are. If we are overweight, and this makes us unhappy, the unhappiness is more often borne out of the daily images of what the media and society deems to be attractive.

It we look in the mirror and are unhappy with what we see and how we think we look, that is our perception of what others think, when in reality others often have different ideas. If we are unhappy with our homes, our lives, our jobs, there may be external reasons , of course, but we may sometimes need to look at our expectations as well. We are who we are, yes, with all of us there is room for improvement , none of us are perfect, but we are loved as we are, that is the bottom line.

When I reached this conclusion, as the walls had completely crumbled around me I realised that there are no ifs, no buts, no maybes. Fact, we are loved as we are . This revelation began a process of stripping layer after layer after layer, not of my faith and belief system but rather the negative teachings surrounding it. I was left with a road ahead of me, a path to tread. It is a road I am journeying along with so many others a road where God is no longer in a box and is found in nature, the sea, the moon, the stars, the wind the rain the thunder, the lightening, in a glass of wine, a meal, a touch, a whisper, a smile, the trees, the leaves, the love. God is , for me, Freedom.

I am not confined to one mode of interpretation, one way. Yes, I make sense of it all predominately in terms of the teachings, life and message of Jesus, but I meet God in other human interpretations, most profoundly in Druidism, but also in every religion. The bottom line is that this is all religion tries to do – make sense of God.

A self help guide to freedom.

When I was first Ordained I made a clear commitment in my mind to only do those things within a church service that had a clear meaning and whose meaning I could explain. I cringe now at some of the practices that I bought into. Yes, I could and can explain their meaning, and where appropriate and meaningful to those I minister to I will use them, but on a personal level, without the walls the meaning is , well, meaningless.

I don't know who you are, I don't know why you have picked up this book. Curiosity, perhaps? You have reached this point and you may have enjoyed it, I may have angered you, even upset you, if I have , I am sorry that was never my intention. You may be jumping up and down and thinking "YES" , you may be about to discard it altogether. I have shared my life, my journey, I have bared my soul to you, and now what I want to do is to just give you a little send off on your own journey, if it is a spiritual journey that you wish to take. The following "self help" guide is a very basic version of the Spiritual Journey courses that we offer on a one-to-one basis. We understand that for some people there are a whole host of reasons why they wish to look at their Spirituality on their own, and so we offer this very basic insight into how this might be done.

We are all spiritual to a greater or lesser degree. Those who search for a deeper meaning to life do so in a number of ways:

We may attend a religious group to listen to what they believe and have to offer.

We might read books, trawl the internet or research Spiritual paths. Perhaps we have friends who follow a particular religion or path and that appeals to us.

We might have had experiences, feelings, a sixth sense, a "god moment".

Many people these days have experienced a search to a greater or lesser degree with a combination of all these things. Whilst it is becoming less common , some people grow up in a family who follow a particular faith understanding and there are expectations to conform.

Your faith journey is YOUR faith journey. We are social beings and value the support of others , we enjoy sharing and experiencing together. Having said that YOU are unique and your relationship with the Divine is unique, no one else will have the same relationship or exactly the same combination of values and beliefs. This is important to remember as the goal of many religious groups is to get you to sign up to their way of thinking.

Whether you have come from an established faith background , or have had some experience of faith groups you will no doubt have come across a good number of ideas, thoughts and formulas relating to belief structures. This will be a positive but also a negative asset to you. Many of us have "received" faith and Spirituality, it makes sense to us because it has of course been "sold" to us. When I was at university , I was trained in "Christian Apologetics", this is the technical term for not only arguing in favour of the Christian faith, but also for giving the "right" answers. In essence it is a sales technique. Most religious groups who seek converts have a similar discipline and will claim that their way is the right way, convincing you as such with some pretty solid arguments.

A good starting point in establishing where you are is to write down your Spiritual Autobiography. There is no right or wrong way to do this.

Sometimes the best way is just to write away, to talk about what has come to you, what has influenced you and what you believe. I have always found that just doing this, without any pre planning can, in the very process of writing, unearth long forgotten moments and interactions which ultimately may be key to who we are. This is not something that can be rushed. It is something, when working with others , we ask them to do over the course of a number of weeks. You won't remember everything, but it's good to try to record highlights.

Once you have completed this process, try to extract some of the key areas in relation to what you have believed along your journey and why. Were these beliefs experiential? Were they taught? Did they make sense to you at the time/ do they make sense now? Then begin to ask yourself why you have believed do believe these things. Try to look deeply at what you believe. If what you believe forms the basis of a religious dogma or creed , think
beyond the temptation to say "the holy book / the pastor says so." For example, the Christian Lord's prayer might be important to you as an expression of your belief system. The opening words, "Our Father, who art in heaven", could be special to you and could form an important part of your faith. Do you believe that God is understood as "father" , do you believe he is in "heaven" ? If so, what do you believe heaven to be, try to rationalise it.

Do some research on what others say about your beliefs. For example, if part of your make up is say from a Wicca background, what is Wicca from other people's perspectives (look at it from, say, a Christian perspective – you will be surprised at some of the ignorance that you will come across). Then spend some time writing down and examining your own values, a value is something which is important to you, examples might be things like, "All life is sacred, that is why I am a pacifist and vegetarian, Abortion is permitted in certain circumstances, Marriage is not a legal contract but rather a recognition by society that a commitment has been made and thus can be conducted anywhere...."

By this stage you will not only have a wealth of material about yourself, but you may have found you have ventured into areas of your life that you have not really considered before. Go back and read through everything you have written, trying to do so from an open perspective, i.e. if your background is predominately Christian, try to read your words without a bias towards what you have been taught is right.

Finally, and this is the most important part of the journey, define God. This is perhaps the most difficult part of all for some, explaining who God is in relation to your own life experience. From your experiences, try to explain not only who God is, but the personality of God. For example, is God in your mind close, distant, loving, concerned with you? Do you feel that invoking certain rituals brings you into closer contact with God, for example praying, going to sacred places, chanting, lighting candles, burning incense?

Is God "up there" or is God here, do you experience God in the leaves, the wind, the trees, the rain, the sea, the fields, the smiles and love of others?

Throughout this whole process, try to avoid being influenced by others or by the spiritual walls you have already built up around you. Keep an open mind at all times and when you have reached this point you will find that you have an understanding of God that is unique to you, to your relationship with God and which will ultimately be the foundation stone of your journey. You may find yourself in a Christian place, in a Buddhist place, connecting with Paganism, Spiritualism or Druidism, of indeed any combination of these traditional spiritualities. The key is to then grow, once you have found God and found your path, walk it. It can be helpful to walk with others who are like minded , but a word of caution, so many religious groups, faith gatherings and spiritual expressions, however open they may claim to be have walls which they will caution you not to go near , and woe betide you if you cross them. If you want to link up with and journey with others choose carefully, allow these groups to enrich your journey and to deepen your experience of God, but at the same time look out for signs that might take you on a narrower path, teachings that are absolute, threats of being "outside" if you take a particular viewpoint, and most importantly "this is the way things are done".

Religion , far from bringing life, so often brings slavery to a belief system that we are not fully in agreement with and far from allowing us to grow and be the person God has created us to be we become two different people, our real private self and our different public face. To be ourselves we need to be free, we need to allow ourselves to grow and to make our own choices.

Your walls no longer exist, your journey has begun, and alongside so many others who have embraced free

Spiritual paths you have begun the process of finding yourself, of connecting with the world around you at a much deeper level and of finding God.

You are Free.

" The most important kind of freedom is to be what you really are. You trade in your reality for a role. You trade in your sense for an act. You give up your ability to feel, and in exchange, put on a mask."

Jim Morrison 1943 – 1971

Postscript

I remain, and always will be a Christian Priest, that is my vocation, that is my calling, and that is the charge that was given to me when hands were laid upon me. However I am not a Priest of any particular Christian denomination , and as such I am not required or compelled to teach or adhere to any particular shade of Christianity , nor do I need to label myself as "catholic" ," protestant" etc. Indeed the label "Christian" disturbs me these days. I follow Jesus the Nazarene, not the teachings of the Church, or the rantings of St. Paul. My Priesthood is rather about living by the teachings and message of Jesus, a message of Love, forgiveness, freedom and justice, and of sharing that message in every interaction with others.

I can celebrate the Sacraments, dispenses blessings, pronounce absolution, exorcise demons and all those things which the Church has seen fit to empower their Priests to do, but it doesn't make me any different from you, or anyone for that matter. I am a simple soul who has always been a square peg in a round hole, never comfortable with conformity, with belief systems that are absolute, which exclude or condemn. The road to this point has been a long, painful, joyful and complicated one, but when I look back one that has been worth every tear. Freedom to be who I am is exhilarating, life giving and enriching. However, freedom cannot be something where we sit watch the beauty around us, we need to keep walking.

Printed in Great Britain
by Amazon